A Gift from
Mr. Ted Girard

Junior Science
spiders

Terry Jennings

Illustrations by David Anstey

Gloucester Press
New York · London · Toronto · Sydney

About this book

You can learn many things about spiders in this book. It tells you how spiders make webs and catch their prey, what happens to their eggs, and where spiders like to live. There are lots of activities and experiments for you to try. You can find out how to make a home for a house spider and how to find out if spiders like the dark or the light best.

First published in the
United States in 1989 by
Gloucester Press
387 Park Avenue South
New York, NY 10016

ISBN 0 531 17176 0

Library of Congress Catalog
Card Number: 88-83614

© BLA Publishing Limited 1989

This book was designed and produced by BLA
Publishing Limited, TR House, Christopher
Road, East Grinstead, Sussex, England.
A member of the Ling Kee Group
London Hong Kong Taipei Singapore New York

Printed in Spain by Heraclio Fournier, S.A.

All spiders have eight legs. They also have two main parts to their bodies. There is a little "waist" between these two parts of the body.

The animals in the picture were all found in a yard. Can you tell which ones are spiders? There are only two spiders. They are labelled D and G.

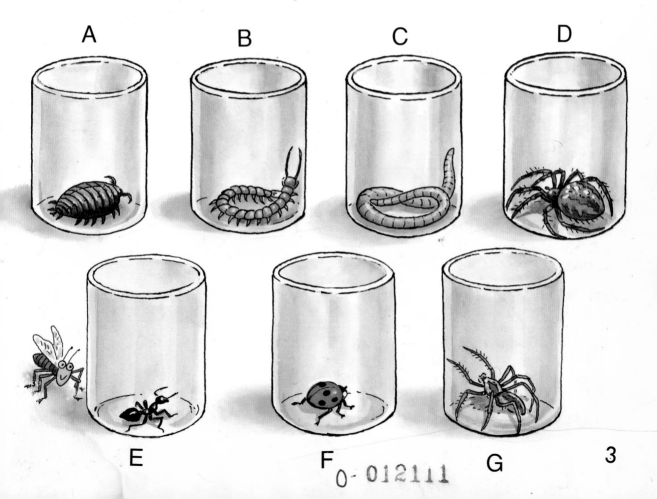

A   B   C   D

E   F   G   3

There are many different kinds of spiders. Some are large and others are so small you can hardly see them.

Many spiders make a sticky web out of silk.

This is the web of a garden spider. A line of silk runs from the web to a hiding place nearby. The spider waits there. When an insect flies into the web, the spider runs out and ties up the insect in silk. Then the spider kills the insect and eats it.

A garden spider starts its web with a line of silk. The line joins two plants or twigs. Then the spider adds two more lines. The web is now shaped like the letter Y. After this the spider makes a frame for the web. Then the other parts of the web are added.

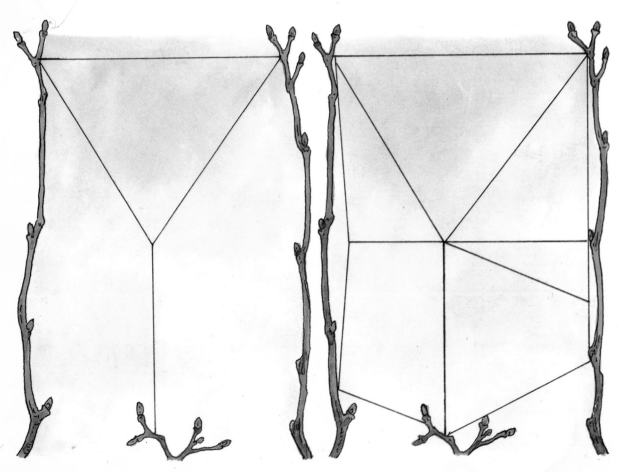

6

Look at a spider web with a magnifying glass. You will see little blobs on the lines of the web. These blobs are a sticky substance which traps insects. If you touch the web gently with a piece of grass, the spider will come running out to see what it is.

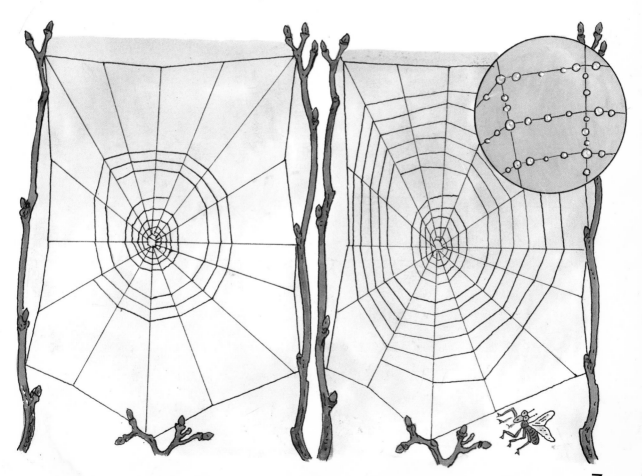

House spiders live in houses and other buildings. The house spider's web is like a sheet of silk. The spider sits in a corner of its web and waits for insects to come along.

You may have found a house spider in your bathtub. They sometimes go there to drink water.

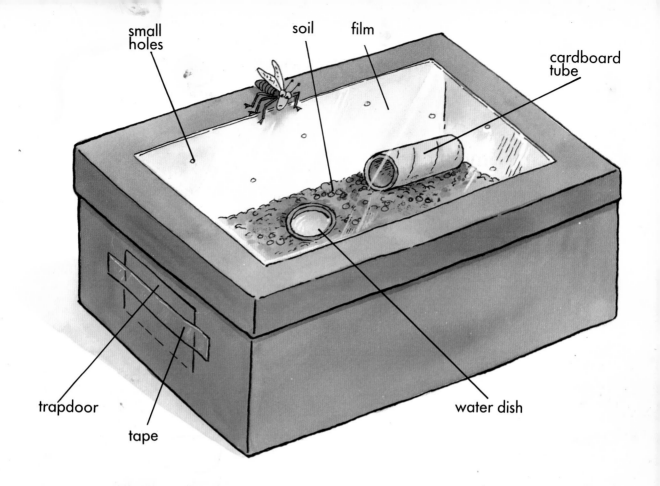

small holes

soil

film

cardboard tube

trapdoor

tape

water dish

You can make a home for a house spider like this.
Take a shoe box and set it up like the one in the
picture. The spider will make a web. Put flies in the
box. They will become trapped in the web and the
spider will eat them. After you have watched your
spider for a little while, set it free again.

9

This boy wanted to collect some spiders' webs.
When he found a web, he cut a piece of black
cardboard a bit larger than the web. He wanted to
attach the web to his cardboard, so he put some
glue all the way around the edge. Then he put the
cardboard behind the web and brought it forward so
that the web stuck to it. Afterward he wrote on the
cardboard when and where he had found the web.

10

Then the boy tried to make a web
from string. You can see the web
he made in the picture below.
The boy's web is not good
enough to catch flies.

Many spiders lay their eggs in the fall. The garden spider does this. The female hides her eggs in cracks in wood or tree bark. She wraps them in a silk bag.

This girl found a spider's egg bag on a fence. She put it in a jar. She covered the jar with a piece of old pantyhose and looked at the eggs every day.

In the spring, tiny spiders hatched from the eggs. The girl stood a twig in the jar. The baby spiders climbed up the twig. Each baby spider was carried away by the wind. The baby spiders could then find a place to make their own webs.

13

Not all spiders make webs. Some hide under bark or stones or in long grass. Wolf spiders like the one in the picture do this. So do the tarantulas of Europe. These spiders chase insects. They have good eyesight and use this to find their prey.

wolf spider with her ball of eggs

14

baby spiders

Not all spiders leave their eggs. The female wolf spider lays her eggs in a ball of silk. She carries the silk ball around on her back. Tiny spiders hatch from the eggs. They ride around on their mother's back until they can care for themselves.

This boy looked in the garden for wolf spiders. He searched in long grass, under stones and pieces of wood. He put the stones and wood back where he found them. At last he found a female wolf spider with a ball of eggs. He gently put the spider in a jar.

Then he made a cage for the spider like this. He gave the spider flies to eat and looked at it every day. When the eggs hatched, the boy watched the baby spiders with a magnifying glass. He let all his spiders go in some long grass.

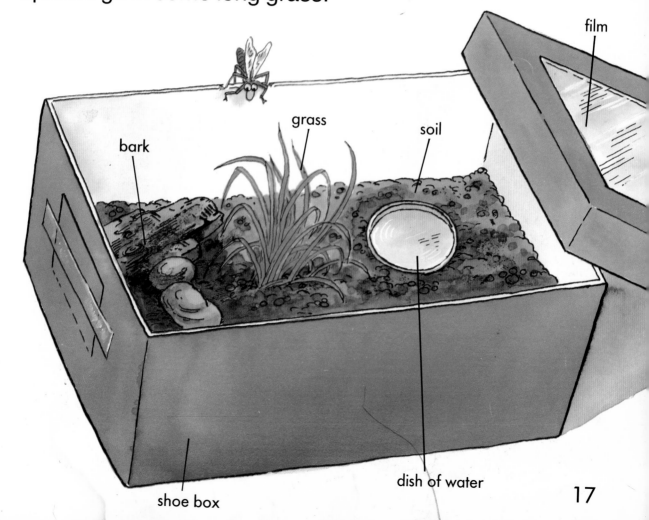

film

grass

soil

bark

dish of water

shoe box

Try this experiment to see if house spiders like the light or the dark best. Take a plastic toothbrush tube and carefully cut the ends off it. Put black paper around half of the tube. Then put it in a box with a house spider in it.

Cover the box with plastic wrap and make small holes in the wrap so that the spider can breathe. Put the box on a window sill and see which part of the tube the spider hides in. It will hide in the dark part of the tube because spiders like to rest in darkness best.

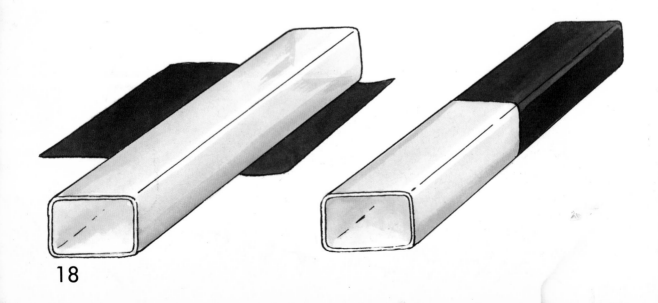

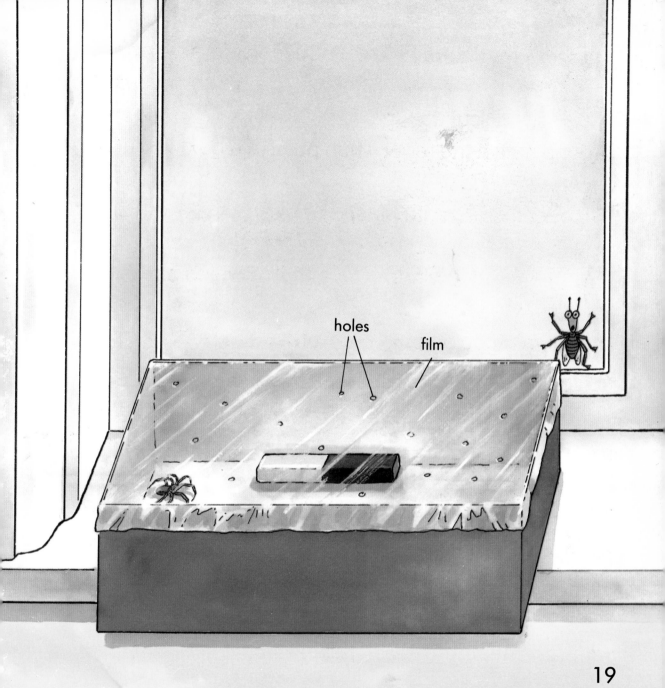

holes

film

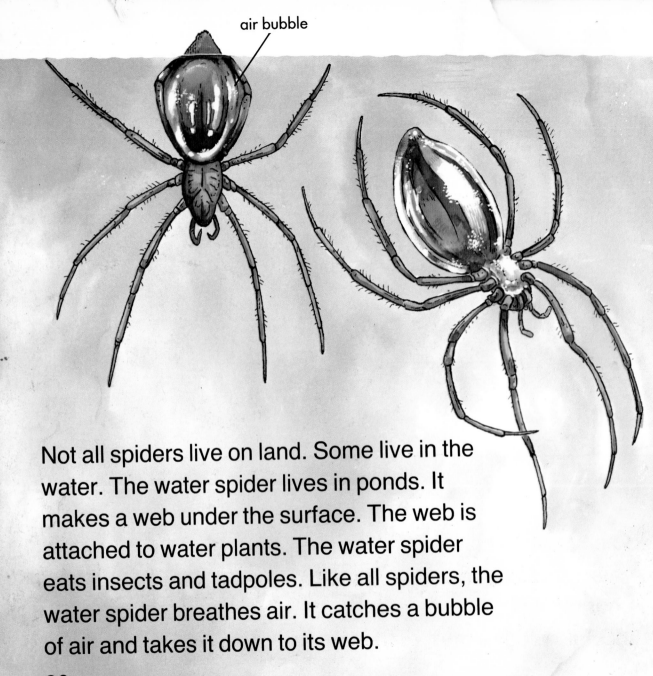

air bubble

Not all spiders live on land. Some live in the water. The water spider lives in ponds. It makes a web under the surface. The web is attached to water plants. The water spider eats insects and tadpoles. Like all spiders, the water spider breathes air. It catches a bubble of air and takes it down to its web.

The spider keeps doing this until its web is full of air bubbles. The spider can then breathe under water. When it has used up all the air, the spider goes back to the surface for more.

Most spiders cannot hurt people. They are much too small. The only really dangerous spiders are black widow spiders. A black widow spider is only about half an inch long. Its bite is very painful, and sometimes it kills. Large hairy spiders called tarantulas live in Europe and North and South America. Their bite can be painful.

glossary

Here are the meanings of some words you may have used for the first time in this book.

dangerous: something that can harm you.

female: any person or animal that can become a mother.

hatch: to break out of an egg.

prey: an animal hunted, killed and eaten by another animal.

silk: a fine thread made by silkworms, spiders and certain other small animals.

spider: a small animal, with two parts to its body and eight legs, which can make silken threads.

surface: the outside of something.

web: a net of fine silken threads spun by a spider.

index